CHRISTIAN
CLIP ART BOOK

Kalishia Winston

us. God is love. If v
will stay

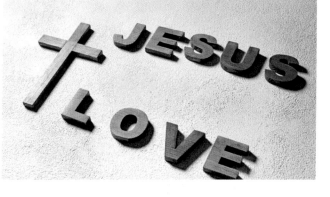

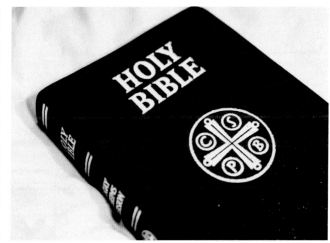

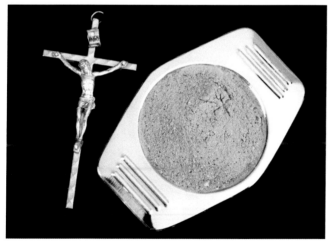

HAVE A BLESSED GOOD FRIDAY

GOOD FRIDAY

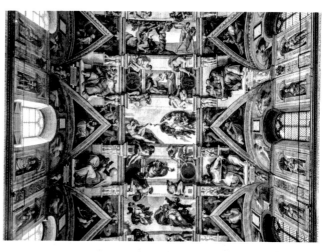

Nothing is
impossible
with God!

Luke 1:37

Be
FIRM
in the
FAITH

Corinthians 16:13-14

In the beginning
God created
the heavens and
the earth.

Genesis 1:1

You are
Loved

God so loved YOU
that he gave his son . . .

John 3:16

If you
BELIEVE
you will receive
whatever you ask
for in
PRAYER

Matthew 21:22

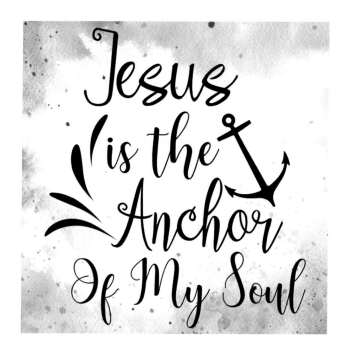

JESUS	FAMILY	EASTER
BLESSED	PRAYER	BELIEVE
FAITH	HOPE	HOLY SPIRIT
BIBLE	FORGIVE	GOOD FRIDAY
PEACE	ASH WEDNESDAY	TRUST
PRAISE GOD	REDEMPTION	RESURRECTION
SERVANT OF GOD	HAPPY	GOD
CHRIST	LOVE	LENT
REPENTANCE	LEARN	SAVIOR
COVENANT	HEAVEN	CHRISTMAS
SAINT	CHRISTIAN	CHURCH

Made in the USA
Las Vegas, NV
03 October 2023

78511479R00021